DATE DUE

HIGHSMITH 45231

Using Energy at Home and School

Andrew Einspruch

Smart Apple Media
P.O. Box 3263
Mankato, MN, 56002

First published in 2010 by
MACMILLAN EDUCATION AUSTRALIA PTY LTD
15–19 Claremont St, South Yarra, Australia 3141

Visit our web site at www.macmillan.com.au or go directly to www.macmillanlibrary.com.au

Associated companies and representatives throughout the world.

Library of Congress Cataloging-in-Publication Data

Einspruch, Andrew.
    Using energy at home and school / Andrew Einspruch.
       p. cm. — (Living sustainably)
    Includes index.
    ISBN 978-1-59920-555-7 (library binding)
    1. Dwellings—Energy conservation—Juvenile literature. 2. School buildings—Energy conservation
    —Juvenile literature. I. Title.
    TJ163.5.D86E365 2011
    644—dc22
                            2009045101

Publisher: Carmel Heron   Designer: Kerri Wilson (cover and text)
Managing Editor: Vanessa Lanaway   Page layout: Kerri Wilson
Editor: Laura Jeanne Gobal   Photo Researcher: Jes Senbergs (management: Debbie Gallagher)
Proofreader: Helena Newton   Illustrator: Robert Shields
                                           Production Controller: Vanessa Johnson

Manufactured in China by Macmillan Production (Asia) Ltd.
Kwun Tong, Kowloon, Hong Kong
Supplier Code: CP January 2010

Acknowledgments

The author and the publisher are grateful to the following for permission to reproduce copyright material:

Front cover photograph of an environmental show and tell, courtesy of © Image Source/Corbis.

Photographs courtesy of © Marc Garanger/Corbis, 10 (bottom); © Image Source/Corbis, 27; Rob Cruse, 3, 5, 17, 18; Shannon Fagan/Getty Images, 25; John Humble/Getty Images, 24; Lisa Romerein/Getty Images, 16; Peter Ziminski/Getty Images, 4; iStockphoto, 10 (left); © Rob Belknap/iStockphoto, 8; © Ian Bracegirdle/iStockphoto, 9; © Gene Chutka/iStockphoto, 6; © Terrance Emerson/iStockphoto, 10 (top right); © David Hernandez/iStockphoto, 21; © Bonnie Jacobs/iStockphoto, 30; © Ruud de Man/iStockphoto, 20; Newspix/News Ltd/Jake Nowakowski, 28; Pelamis, 13; Photolibrary © David Crausby/Alamy, 12; Photolibrary © Martin Shields/Alamy, 22; Photolibrary © David Taylor/Alamy, 26; Photolibrary © Peter Widmann/Alamy, 19; Photolibrary © Michael Willis/Alamy, 23; © Gary 718/Shutterstock, 7; © Angelo Gilardelli/Shutterstock, 11 (right); © Hal.P/ Shutterstock, 11 (bottom left); © Laura Gangi Pond/Shutterstock, 11 (top left); Kim Ward, 29.

While every care has been taken to trace and acknowledge copyright, the publisher tenders their apologies for any accidental infringement where copyright has proved untraceable. Where the attempt has been unsuccessful, the publisher welcomes information that would redress the situation.

Contents

When a word is printed in **bold**, you can look up its meaning in the Glossary on page 31.

Living Sustainably

Living sustainably means using things carefully so there is enough left for people in the future. To live sustainably, we need to look after Earth and its **resources**.

If we cut down too many trees now, there will not be enough lumber in the future.

The things we do make a difference. We can use water, energy, and other resources wisely. Our choices can help make a sustainable world.

Switching the light off when we leave a room is a simple action that makes a difference.

Using Energy at Home and School

We use energy at home and school to power our computers and light our rooms. Energy heats and cools things. We need energy to make almost everything we use and eat.

Without energy, we would not be able to play games on the television.

What Is Energy?

Energy is power. Power is needed for things to work. Different kinds of energy are needed to do different kinds of work. Heat, light, and electricity are examples of energy.

Electricity powers lights in cities around the world.

Where Does Energy Come From?

The energy we use comes from nature. For example, wood can be burned to create heat or light. **Fossil fuels**, such as coal, oil, and natural gas, can also be burned for energy.

Coal is a fossil fuel that has to be dug out of the ground.

Burning Fossil Fuels

Fossil fuels are our main source of energy, but burning fossil fuels releases unwanted **greenhouse gases**. These gases are a form of **pollution**. They are harmful to the **environment**.

Harmful gases are being released by this **power plant**, which is burning coal.

Renewable and Nonrenewable Energy

Some sources of energy are more sustainable than others. Energy from these sources is called renewable energy. Renewable energy does not run out because nature always creates more.

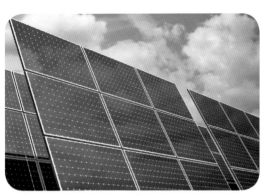

solar energy from the sun

wind energy

The sun, wind, and water are sources of renewable energy.

water energy

Other sources of energy do not last. Once they are used up, nature does not create more. We call these sources nonrenewable energy.

Gasoline, propane, and electricity are made from **fossil fuels**, which are nonrenewable energy sources.

Electricity

Electricity is a very useful kind of energy. It powers lights, refrigerators, and some stoves and ovens. Electricity also powers furnaces and air conditioners. Electricity helps make life comfortable.

How many items in this picture are powered by electricity?

How Is Electricity Created?

Electricity is created at power plants. Some power plants burn coal, oil, or natural gas to create electricity. Other power plants use the sun, wind, or water to create electricity.

This wave farm in Portugal changes the movement of ocean waves into electricity.

How Does Electricity Get to a Wall Plug?

Electricity is sent from a power plant to homes and buildings by power lines.

A power plant creates electricity.

Electricity travels across the country on power lines.

From power lines, electricity is transferred to smaller distribution lines along streets.

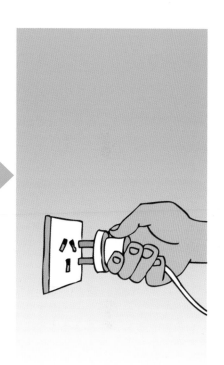

Wires take the electricity inside houses and buildings to wall plugs.

Using Energy Sustainably

If everyone uses energy sustainably, there will always be enough of it. We can use nonrenewable energy sustainably by saving it. We can also replace it with renewable energy.

Natural gas, which is often used when cooking, is a nonrenewable energy source.

Saving energy means using less electricity and natural gas. The easiest way to save energy is to turn things off when they are not being used.

Save electricity by turning off or unplugging electronic devices at the wall plug instead of leaving them on "standby."

Save Energy in the Kitchen

We can save energy in the kitchen by closing doors. Close the refrigerator door to keep the cold inside. Close the oven door to keep the heat inside.

When doors are closed, less energy is used to keep things hot or cold.

We can also save energy in the kitchen by:
- closing the kitchen door to keep cold or hot air out when the furnace or air conditioner is running
- washing dishes in a dishwasher or dishpan because less water will have to be heated

Microwaves use less energy than ovens and work faster, too.

Save Energy in the Bathroom

To save energy in the bathroom, take short showers. Short showers use less hot water than baths. The less hot water we use, the less energy is needed to heat it.

Timers can help us keep track of how long we have been in the shower.

Washing our hands in cold water saves the energy needed to heat water.

We can also save energy in the bathroom by:
- switching off the light when we leave the bathroom
- washing our hands with cold water
- filling the bathtub only halfway if we want to have a bath

Save Energy in the Living Room

To save energy in the living room, turn things off when they are not being used. Televisions, stereos, DVD players, and other electronic devices use a lot of electricity.

Energy-saving lightbulbs last longer and use less energy.

Energy Vampires

Energy vampires are things that pretend to be turned off. They are really on "standby" and still using energy. Many electronic devices are energy vampires with red standby lights.

Energy vampires must be unplugged to stop them from using electricity.

Save Energy at School

The ways we save energy at home can be practiced at school, too. If we turn off lights and computers, the school will use less electricity.

Be an energy saver and turn the lights off when the classroom is empty.

Using natural light means no electricity is used to light the classroom.

We can also save energy at school by:
- using sunlight to light the room when possible
- closing curtains and blinds on hot days to keep the sun out
- opening windows and doors to allow the breeze in to cool the classroom on a hot day

Form an Energy Team

Ask your teacher if your school can form an energy team. One teacher and some students from every class could form the team.

Some schools have installed devices which keep track of the school's energy use.

At energy-team meetings, members share ideas for saving energy. Members also report back to their classmates on what they learned at the meetings.

It is important to share ideas on saving energy so that everyone can do it.

Share the Message

Being **energy-smart** is an important message to share with your friends. Ask your teacher if your class can make posters about saving energy to put up around the school.

Share the message about saving energy with fun posters.

An Energy-smart School

Students at Byletts Combined School, South Africa, calculated their computers's electricity use for a year. To make up for the greenhouse gases released when this electricity was created, they planted trees.

Planting trees and other plants makes up for the energy used by computers in a school.

A Sustainable World

Saving energy is one way to live sustainably.
How many ways can you save energy today?
Your choices and actions will help make a
sustainable world.

Make a list of the things you can do every day to use
energy sustainably.

Glossary

energy-smart   acting in a way that helps to save energy

environment   the air, water, and land that surround us

fossil fuels   the buried remains of plants and animals that form fuels such as oil, coal, and natural gas after millions of years

greenhouse gases   gases found in the air that trap heat around Earth and cause higher temperatures

pollution   waste that damages the air, water, or land

power plant   a factory that produces electricity by burning fossil fuels or by using energy from the sun, wind, or water

resources   useful things found on Earth that are hard to replace once they run out

Index